How Angels Fly

How Angels Fly

J. L. Montera

*We members of the Guardian Angel Society
hope to remind you that we are just at
the surface of your remembrance.
Please call on us in need.
Thank us in quiet moments.
We are forever here to serve.*

Storytelling
with
JLM's Garden LLC

Copyright 2015 J. L. Montera

ISBN: 978-0-9967984-0-2
JLM's Garden, LLC
Loveland, Colorado
jlmsgarden.com

Wing Designs © 2015
Meghan Lindquist / mcl42595@gmail.com
Morgan Lindquist / mel42595@gmail.com

Printed in the United States of America

Brendon,

I Love You Forever and Ever and Always

In our particular place in time, a sense of family, remembrance, dialogue, and written or oral history have developed into priceless possessions. Native American storytellers remind us to embrace these possessions and share them with future generations as meaningful legend. Each generation grows as we put into words times past. We learn that we do have value and that we do indeed matter.

I wandered into the study looking for you. You were six and had been quiet for some time—a natural alarm to a grandmother. You were bent over a piece of scrap paper, pencil in one hand and your other hand tapping lightly on the desk. I leaned down to see what you were concentrating on. It was a pencil drawing of an angel.

"Grandma," you said. "I can't get these lines to work."

"What are you trying to draw?" I asked.

"I want to put these on the guardian angel's foot."

Looking at your sketch I saw "these" were a number of lines drawn this way and that. They looked like upside-down triangles and slanting lines. "I'm sure you'll figure it out," I said as I left the room.

"Grandma," you yelled a few minutes later. "I've got it, come and see."

I saw your bright smile as I entered the room. "Wow, that looks great," I said looking at your finished drawing. The random lines had come together and were now positioned inside the angel's foot. "What is that?" I asked, pointing to the design.

"Oh! That is called a symbol."

"Really," I answered wondering how you even knew what a symbol was. "What does it stand for?"

"The symbol says 'Keep Us In Peace.' "

"How do you know that?"

"My guardian angel told me."

For a fleeting moment, I felt the presence of this angel protector and chills ran down my spine. I sat next to you, hugged you, and then asked you to tell me all about your guardian angel.

And so you did. At that very moment, a new storyteller began to weave his contribution to our meaningful legend.

Artist: Brendon

Heaven

It is early morning on earth, business as usual in heaven.

God's chief seraphs, the Archangels, were given His Call to assemble Guardian Angels numbered 103 through 130. In heaven these angels are known as GAs. They serve in the Guardian Angel Society and number in the millions. Heaven's celestial hierarchy has within its purview the task to dispense GAs' Numbers, confirm forthcoming assignments in heaven, track GAs allocated to earth, and more importantly, help God follow the comings and goings of His minions.

Each of the GAs gathered flutter about as they wait, their wings creating a torrent of air that causes the smallest GAs to cast about as they struggle to maintain their positions in the flock. The din is overpowering. The noise resembles that of fighter jets propelled from the deck of an aircraft carrier.

Hovering outside the cluster, a somewhat clumsy guardian angel named GA~105 darts to and fro. He doesn't enter the group because his mismatched wings cause him to wobble.

He wonders why an inept novice like himself has been included in the *Call.* He is certain he will not be chosen as a sentry for a child, an advocate to parents, a guard over teenage impulses, a conscience for a bully, an intention to heal for the ill, a spiritual guide to the dying or any other important task.

∀
GA~105
Heaven

All around him heavenly communication reveals that the life-spans of the earthborn companions to GA~128 and GA~130 have ended. At first light they had gathered their companions' souls, encircled them with their fine-looking wings and returned them to God's home.

Guardian Angels 111, 116, 118 and 119—legendary storytellers in heaven—are retelling of their encounters on earth...

GA~119 states—with conviction—"Complex! That's what it is to serve our earthbound companions when they've forgotten their childlike connection to God."

GA~116 offers, "Our voice is heard in the quiet of their sleep but they forget on waking."

GA~111 adds, "But Heaven's Rules cannot be communal nor—

Interrupting, GA~122 states boldly, "My elderly earthborn said I smelled like ripened strawberries!"

Spreading wide beautiful wings GA~108 affirms, "My smell was lavender."

GA~103 offers, "Motor oil."

$$\forall$$
GA~105
Heaven
3

At this the Guardian Angels collectively laughed so hard they had to extend their wings to full size to keep from shooting off.

God eavesdropped on this exchange and reflected on the qualities of His guardian angels: spiritual creatures with intelligence and will; without ego; sometimes impractical; individual and immortal; loyal protectors, and as close as thought or prayer.

Proclamations and gyrating wings were instantly brought to a standstill as God's ethereal breath encircled those gathered. The richness of His sacred voice quieted all thought. The instant was etched into the character of the collective and a sacred moment passed unnoticed on earth. Soon one GA would be selected as a companion for the lifetime safekeeping of an earthborn.

God's vital breath wove its way to GA~105's spirit. Astounded, 105 could not believe he, an aspiring guardian angel, had been chosen. The news of God's choice spread throughout Heaven's Gates. Those nearby swished past 105 giving him pats on the head and offering best wishes as they departed for their heavenly to-do lists.

Whish! Whish! GA~105 clumsily flapped his mismatched wings in excitement. With great effort he attempted to coordinate them, but in doing so 105 started to tumble about. He flapped harder and harder, which only made matters worse.

Using the air current created by beautiful, elegant wings, GA~108 hovered beneath 105 until he regained control. Embarrassed; he thought how he wished to one day learn how other GAs fly so flawlessly.

An ancient professorial-looking angel—even by heavenly standards—touched 105's shoulder. The contact instantly calmed 105's embarrassment, excitement, confusion and concerns. His wings, without effort, folded into place. God observed professor and student with deep affection.

The ancient one, Professor Thistle, was not a guardian angel, nor did he have wings. This fact disappointed GA~105 as he wondered, *"How will I learn to fly if my professor has no wings?"* With instant regret for this unkind thought, 105 lowered his head

∀
GA~105
Heaven
5

and followed his professor to heaven's Guardian Angel Classroom. Entering the classroom GA~105 declared, "Professor, I don't believe I am ready to take on an earthborn. I cannot fly and I have no qualifications to speak of. Perhaps this is a mistake."

Professor Thistle with empathy in his voice replied, "I will do all within my power to minister to your anxiety and doubt. You will be ready, I promise."

Guardian Angel Classroom
Assignment Number One

The assignment required GA~105 to write a thank-you note to God for choosing him for earthborn work. He didn't know how he could put words to the sentiments lying deep in his spirit: thankfulness, fear, and a willingness to serve.

"How do I address God?"

"Ah," said Professor Thistle, "that is a question only you can answer. God hears each of us in our own unique way. He relishes our prayers and warms to our inflections. He will know your heart, regardless of your words."

∀

GA~105

Heaven

6

Father of My Being,

You honor me, and it is with humility that I write this thank-you note. My soul is bursting with gratitude but words are useless to illustrate. When I make mistakes I will be accountable. When I fall I will get up. I will pray each day for your guidance and I ask that you bless my journey.

Respectfully,
Guardian Angel~105

Professor Thistle bowed his head and folded his hands in prayer. Finally he spoke, "You are a blessing to God, to the Guardian Angel Society, and especially to the earthborn you will protect."

Many more months of instruction followed between Professor Thistle and GA~105—six earth months to be exact—before 105 finally asked, "Am I ready?"

"Not quite," responded Professor Thistle. He continued, "Each first-time, earthbound GA is required to compose a message to the parents of their lifelong earthly companion. You may research samples of these messages in the Holy Library, where all knowledge is stored. But know that your message must be as original as the earthborn you are to protect. When finished, your one-of-a-kind message will be added to Heaven's everlasting tome entitled *Angel Thoughts*. With God's blessing, this book will remain open until the end of time."

The Holy Library, with floor-to-ceiling shelves, displayed hardbound books with multihued covers and tattered pages. The wide-ranging collection included gigantic leather-bound volumes with jagged spines and miniature parchment booklets tied with silk thread. Each section is labeled: Handwritten Journals, Fiction, Nonfiction, Real Stories, Aged Stories, Humankind Life Stories, History, Medicine, Mystery, Geography, and Physics, to name a few. The sample *Angel Thoughts* archives are, as it turns out, at ceiling height, just to the left of the Mystery section.

"May I help you?" asked the angel librarian who robustly swept out of the assigned cubicle. His hefty wings, rounded on top like a basketball, reached the library floor and were naturally spread because of their size.

"I, uh, yes please," replied GA~105. "I need to look at samples of *Angel Thoughts*—but I don't think I can make it to the ceiling without crashing into shelves or—"

Interrupting 105 by floating around him, the librarian investigated the GA's wings then looked from floor to ceiling, winked, and lifted off to retrieve the samples. No time passed—being heaven and all—before the librarian handed the samples to 105. He suggested to 105, without speaking, that he use a nearby ground-level desk for his review.

Three months had passed—as humankind knows it—when Guardian Angel~105 finally handed his assignment to Professor Thistle: the letter to the parents of the earthborn he was to protect. His professor held the letter with his right hand and placed spectacles on his nose with his left. He read aloud:

$$\forall$$
GA~105
Heaven
9

J. L. Montera

Dear Parents,

I have a joyous assignment. It is my thankful duty and blessing to introduce you to the child chosen for your life.

God's touch smolders in your child's soul who ascends through the Light of God to be with you. During the journey, his thoughts were formed about life's fundamental nature to seek these: Human Touch, Comfort, Kindness, Wonderment, Promise, Family, Dreams, Trust, and Conversation. God calls upon you to sculpt the resting place for these thoughts in your child.

Know that you nurture and shape your child by your actions and not your words. It is of equal importance that you honor your commitment to the relationship between you and God.

Affectionately,
Guardian Angel~105

Professor Thistle removed his spectacles, dabbed at tears, and reached across his desk to take 105's essence into his. With great joy, he declared, "You are ready!"

Earth

Without awareness, GA~105 emerged in the nursery of a baby boy named Brendon. He floated above the crib for a moment before he realized he was about to topple over. *I am off to a bad start*, he thought. I, the heaven-sent, am protector of this earthborn for a lifetime and yet I am still a novice.

The nursery door opened, cutting short his worried thoughts. Grandmother Eugenia smelled apple blossoms as she stepped inside the nursery. A warm glow, like a fireplace on a cold evening, enveloped the entire space. Umm, she thought, Brendon's guardian angel must be nearby. Guardian Angel~105 was so startled by her thought he started to descend again. Catching himself, he saw her wipe away tears saying, "Brendon, I will love you forever, and ever, and always."

After a full day of visitors, feedings, a warm bath and swathed in a yellow baby blanket, Brendon slept. Guardian Angel~105 settled in the Light of God that still shown about the baby. He folded his mismatched wings as quietly as possible. Still, they caused a puff of air to move across Brendon's face. "Goodnight and keep us in peace," he prayed. "And God, know that I seek your sanction and guidance."

When Brendon was a little older, just learning to walk, GA~105 was constantly darting from place to place, spreading one wing then the next to guard against sharp edges, all in the name of protector. During these efforts he tried, rarely with success, to match Brendon's movements with ungainly wings for counterbalance. At night, both angel and child were exhausted.

In his sleeping, Brendon questioned the purpose of guardian angels and asked, "How *DO* angels fly anyway?"

Guardian Angel~105 explained to the soul that was Brendon that he too wondered how angels fly. He just wasn't sure. What GA~105 did know, and

∀
GA~105
Earth

shared with Brendon, is that angels come when we sleep to listen to our heart's longings. They answer questions only when asked, and their wings are like that of a butterfly but enhanced for travel beyond space and time. When skilled, their wings open and close with a gentle, controlled flow. When they flutter, warm air moves across any flat surface, complemented by their distinct fragrance. Angels float like puffy afternoon clouds that form when Earth's parcels of air are rising. Angels make use of this source of energy to rest their wings in flight. Each GA carries God's promise to always protect, especially when remembrance of them is mislaid. There is in humankind a burden of growing older and forgetting that, what was, still is and, but one thought away.

A few years later, Brendon was animated as he boasted to his GA that he'd ridden his bicycle many, many times—without needing training wheels. "I'm in kindergarten," he said with great authority. "Our teacher said tomorrow we will ride on a yellow school bus and take something she calls a field trip. We will visit a museum and see dinosaur bones. Did

∀
GA~105
Earth
13

you know that dinosaurs were very, very big and you could hear their roar for miles?"

Guardian Angel~105 began to anticipate how active his day would be following Brendon and staying out of the way of the other guardian angels. "Well," he thought, "we need to get some sleep for the busy day ahead. Goodnight."

"…and keep us in peace," he prayed.

Brendon's guardian angel was realizing that during the last few earth years, as Brendon was growing, so were his own wings. They didn't ache as much and were now shaped more like a backward question mark. His fondness for this earth child was deepening as well.

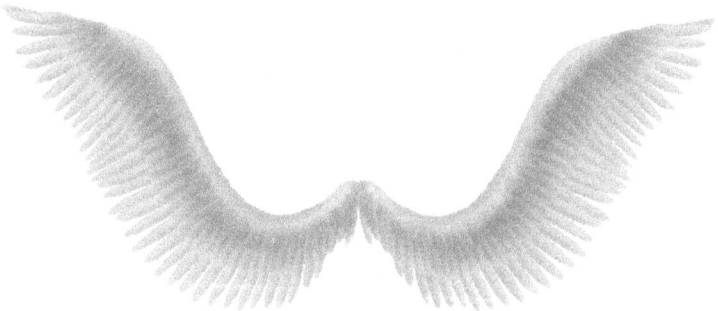

∀
GA~105
Earth

14

Brendon shouted across the hallway at his mother, "Mom, I woke up this morning wondering how angels fly."

"What a strange question for a fifth grader," she yelled back as she dashed downstairs to prepare breakfast.

Brendon stumbled down the stairs after her and declared as he entered the kitchen—his dad already seated with coffee and newspaper in hand—"Hey you guys, you gotta hear my dream. I remember feeling warm air move across my face and the smell of apple blossoms in my room. Have you ever heard the words, 'keep us in peace'?"

"Maybe it's something you ate," his mother responded as she mixed the pancake batter and cracked an egg into a frying pan.

"This local election is in full swing… What was that, son; something about peace? Wouldn't that be nice?"

Years had passed without notice on Earth, but in Heaven each instant had been recorded.

Brendon suddenly found himself pushing back hard against a boy who kept thumping him. He didn't like how angry he felt. The teacher broke it up and asked both boys what happened. Brendon told the truth, the other boy lied. Parents were called. Brendon's punishment was clearly outlined. He was to apologize to the other boy and do extra household chores for a month. He swore he heard the words *keep us in peace* as he lay in bed that night, fuming that he was in trouble just for telling the truth.

Guardian Angel~105's admiration for this young man was growing daily as he watched him struggle to find his identity and his truth. During this same time GA~105's wings had filled in, adding weight and precision. He was now able to cover more ground by distributing his weight evenly while flapping his wings without hurry.

The earth years were a jumble now. Brendon was a 25-year-old man with college behind him and a cadre of good friends. Recently, he'd attended a bachelor party for his best buddy—GA~105 present, as always. There was laughing and drinking and more drinking. Late in the evening, other friends approached Brendon to drive them home. As he dug in his pocket for his car keys, he felt a warm breeze cross his face and the room smelled like apple blossoms. He chalked it up to too many beers. Yet he told his friends, "Let's all bunk here. I'm too tired to drive." That night Brendon dreamt that he saw an angel fly—just the alcohol, he decided.

Guardian Angel~105 could not believe how quickly earth years add up. In Heaven there is no time but on earth... Brendon was forty and the father of three. Grandmother Eugenia had died six months earlier, leaving an emptiness in their lives. She had gifted her home to Brendon and recently he and his family had moved in. Her upstairs bedroom, with its hundred-year-old writing desk, books, rocking chair, and antique bed, had not been disturbed.

It was on a cold December Sunday morning that Brendon climbed the curved staircase and entered his grandmother's bedroom for only the second time since moving into her home.

He opened her writing desk and discovered a collection of journals, ten in all. One in particular caught his eye as it reminded him of her love for the arts. The journal's cover showed a sheet of classical music, two satin-white ballerina slippers, and one withered rose tied together with a long, faded ribbon that hung from a rusty nail. He opened the journal, flipped through a few pages, and saw his name. In his grandmother's hand was written . . .

Brendon,

This is the story of a small child and an old woman, but oh, so much more. I find a peacefulness in its telling and I offer it to you with love.

—Grandmother Eugenia

I will never forget the first time I saw you. You didn't know it was spring or how much I loved you. As I bent down to pick you up, tears of joy and tenderness filled my eyes and heart. You smelled like baby lotion, your room like apple blossoms. I suspicioned your guardian angel was nearby. I watched you grow physically, emotionally, and spiritually. I endured your pain and relished your joy.

Each spring when you visited my home, we had bedtime talks, a much-loved tradition. We discussed the importance of a hug and how to give comfort, perform kind deeds, trust one another, enjoy family, and keep promises.

How Angels Fly

You were three years old when we began our annual spring walks down the curved dirt road toward a clump of apple trees. We held hands then, your small one in mine, which linked us until you darted off on a quest. We stopped to check sparkling rocks, and butterfly moths perched on dandelions. We watched a yellow and black chickadee swooping overhead, a hawk soaring, and deer lying in the shade of a cottonwood. Once, we captured a bull snake and moved it to higher ground. It took months for the smell of that dead skunk to disappear. We looked for wolf spider webs and meadowlark nests in the tall grasses.

Six-year-old boys love adventure, so it didn't surprise me that you wanted to start our walk early that day. The smell of apple blossoms drifted into the sunroom windows and drew us like bees to honey. We strolled hand in hand, unaware of what was ahead.

After the customary time given to exploration, we reached the stately apple trees bursting with flowers. We leaned against the split-rail fence, and I closed my eyes to relish the moment. The smell of lavender crossed my face, carried on a warm breeze. I opened my eyes to a light that almost blinded. Mesmerized, you were staring off over the trees. I saw an immense white butterfly hovering just above the treetops. An unusual hush had fallen over the meadow.

∀
GA~105
Earth

I felt your hand reach for mine, and you dotingly drew me to you. You leaned into me and with a comforting voice said, "Grandmother, I know how angels fly."

The light surrounding us grew brighter. "How?" I asked quickly.

"They fly with their hearts."

Slowly Brendon closed the journal and, embracing it, wept—wept for all he had forgotten.

Guardian Angel~105 spread flawless wings and, embracing Brendon, wept—wept with thankfulness.

∀
GA~105
Earth
20

www.ingramcontent.com/pod-product-compliance
Lightning Source LLC
Chambersburg PA
CBHW030012040426
42337CB00012BA/745